THE
PENITENTES

Janice A. Valdez

BALBOA.
PRESS
A DIVISION OF HAY HOUSE

Balboa Press books may be ordered through booksellers or by contacting:

Balboa Press
A Division of Hay House
1663 Liberty Drive
Bloomington, IN 47403
www.balboapress.com
1 (877) 407-4847

Print information available on the last page.

ISBN: 978-1-9822-2747-0 (sc)
ISBN: 978-1-9822-2750-0 (e)

Library of Congress Control Number: 2019942751

Balboa Press rev. date: 04/30/2019

FOREWORD

I have written this book to share with my familia, extended family, friends and Historians. I want to provide an opportunity to honor those who have come before us and who have shaped our lives and way of living.

There are many things that shape our lives, perhaps our history is the most significant. Yet it is the least understood. In our History classes we are given names of people who have contributed to our history but their role in our lives is a very minor one. We must begin where we were born and raised, those are the people that have influenced our lives more than anyone. They have given us our names and who have fashioned for us a history as beautiful and rich as it is obscure.

I am dedicating my book to my Grandchildren, Elizabeth Duran, Taylor Sophia, Andrew Daniel, Jaelynn Riley, and Bailey Isabella Valdez. They have inspired me though out my years to go on after some terrible tragedies that have occurred to me. They have been my motivation the past twelve years that we have been together. Seeing their smiles every day, and all their achievements have left the most memorable and dazzling effects on my life.

I think my book will attract many walks of life. I think it is quite important for people to read and learn exactly how life was really like when our communities were first formed with firsthand information on how our villages and communities really came about. I think this book could be used in schools and universities for people who are interested how our lives were and still are influenced by our ancestors. Many people do not even know that the Penitentes shaped our ancestors and our lives in many ways.

I would love to preserve this rich culture of our History that existed so many years ago and still affects our lives here today. The Castilian Spanish, morals, values and our rich culture that came with the Penitentes which still exists today but has become unnoticed.

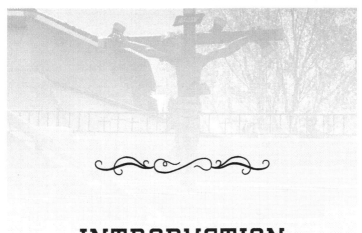

INTRODUCTION

I have great love for preserving and retelling unwritten history that my great-grand parents, grand-parents, parents and my self has lived to tell about. I have great ambition to save our culture and to retell stories of how our ancestors lived. I believe that among the things that shape our lives, perhaps our history is the most significant. I have always had a dream in my mind that someday I would be given the opportunity to be able to retell the stories of our ancestors. I have great hopes that you can help me get this book of the Penitentes published, so many of our people can read this and imagine what our lives were like. I believe this book should be published because what is written in this book is exactly what I witnessed as a child and young adult. I have written what my grandparents, parents shared with me about a way of living that actually was the government of this small villages. That is exactly how they learned to live and follow rules in a civilized world. I have never read a book written about the Penitentes where the author actually saw and or experienced their way of living. Our language and culture has been preserved for hundreds of years because of this secret society. They are the ones that brought the Castilian Spanish to our area. The purpose of this book is to share how our culture, morals, and values were being developed in a very low profile way of living and their way of living by their strong ways still exist in our small rural communities. This book can be read by many different people who have a wide variety of interests. They may be interested in the area or they may want to learn a very different way of how a village functioned many years ago. How the villages were formed and the purpose everyone was responsible for in their individual village. I believe our culture has been denied or wrongly described the real way our villages came about and the real way we have lived in for hundreds of years. I believe my book will attract different people who have interest in culture, ethnics, history, and how the real Hispanics lived hundreds of years ago. A totally different form of government that worked just fine for the people who lived in these areas. I believe my book is unique and very culturally related to all Hispanics.

CONTENTS

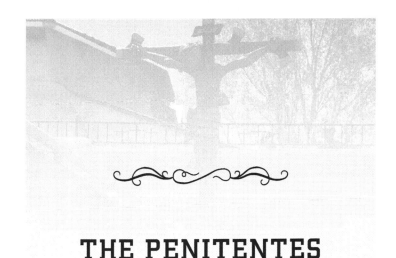

THE PENITENTES

This is a brief history of one of the most fascinating, and misunderstood religious groups in the world. Los Hermanos Penitentes, a Catholic brotherhood found only in Northern New Mexico and Southern Colorado. The Hermanos Penitentes is an organization lacking a written Literary. The History of the Penitentes is got nothing but errors and misinterpretations. Legends and folklore handed down orally over the years, are open to interpretations that are not necessarily correct at all. People from all over the world have been interested in the Penitentes for many years.

As I have gotten older and more mature I have come to realize that there are no written interpretations of what life was like when the Penitentes lived here. I was born and raised in Los Sauces, Colorado. As a young child I remember watching the Hermanos go about their rituals. Across so many Memories and much sympathy and little antipathy here and there, there appears in the eyes of affection a living mosaic, lovely in every way, and pleasant in every way. In it there are beloved figures, deeply felt incidents and accidents, remembered lines and contours. The magical colors that come out thru the sun rays, pebbles that shine, rocks that will frighten you. Changing light and shadow, sometimes revealing, sometimes concealing, according to the sun, or the moon, or the cloud or the mist of a memory. A human landscape, animated and lively appears in the hearts and minds of everyone in this beautiful, palpitating and romantic representation of what one day was the way the Hermano Penitentes lived their lives and governed their communities.

I am surprised to see in that mosaic something I never saw before, a main theme among others. Perhaps distance, age, or tranquility are necessary, in order to see the lilies of the valley. Perhaps one needs a toothache, in order to remember one has teeth. If it doesn't hurt you, you do not notice, and you do not care. The Hermano Penitentes have excited interest in many people traveling thru Northern New Mexico and Southern Colorado.

I never felt the pain of the Penitentes, therefore I never took them seriously, but I have always been very intrigued of what I learned from them. Now much older and wiser, I contemplate the panorama of the past in astonishment and I can see the tremendous importance that the Presence of the Penitentes had on the history of our people. We cannot ignore the influence they had on all of our lives.

HISTORY

In the beginning there was no government in these lands, no church, and no school. The people that lived here did what they could with what they had. The Brotherhood of the Penitentes was the only group with authority, the only disciplined organization in these isolated villages, abandoned first by Spain, later by Mexico and finally by the United States.

In the farthest corner of the civilized world, in this isolation, in this abandonment and almost, total neglect our people could have ended in a state of barbarism. They could have lost their language, their religion and their traditions. They could have lost their civilized ways and could have lost their identity. They could have stopped being Hispanos and because of the Penitentes none of these things happened. After four hundred years Hispanic culture remains alive and alert all because of the Hermano Penitentes, they brought us an organized way of living.

The Penitentes more than anyone filled the administrative, religious, and cultural vacuum. Being the only organized structure where there was no official government they took the initiative in establishing the guidelines of government for the villages, and the strong arm of the brotherhood was always available to maintain public order, the defense of the village and to provide help in disasters. They also provided great political service. The Brotherhood was large and had branches in every village. This served to establish communication, harmony and union among the diverse and scattered villages.

In a world without Priests, the Penitentes kept the religion unblemished. They were the ones that instructed the people in prayer, the ceremonies, and the sacraments, the mysteries and the hymns of the church. They had the books and the manuscript. Through the religious exercises they kept the language alive and relatively pure. Perhaps we owe in large measure the mysticism of characteristic of our people to the Penitentes. So who knows how many of our people have gone to heaven and have introduced themselves to Saint Peter in Perfect Castilian Spanish, thanks to the Penitentes. Most of the few books and manuscripts were in the hands of the Penitentes in colonial times. Consequently, they were among the few who knew how to read and write. The fact that our people did not lose these arts is due in great part to the men of the secret society. A person that can read and write knows how to live and die.

PENITENTES FUNCTIONS

Each Penitente Morada or Chapter is an autonomous entity. It is, therefore, almost impossible to generalize about rites and customs. Some groups emphasize self-flagellation while others rarely make use of the whip. Within every single Morada it was very possible that the rituals would vary from one village to another. They would vary from year to year and from generation to generation.

First of all, it must be understood that Los Hermanos Penitentes did not only appear during lent. They were active societies with charitable works throughout the year. They were especially involved at the death of a member during which they would always supervise the VELORIO (wake) of the person whom had passed on.

Went lent approached they would devote their time to personal and community penance. The members would meet at their Morada (the meeting place for all the Hermanos) on Wednesdays and Fridays during lent. Special services were held in preparation for Holy Week. All during lent, but particularly in Holy Week, there was an orgy of torture and blood. If the penance of self-flagellation is to be performed at any time, the Sangrador makes three slashes on each side of the spine of the Penitentes with a knife or piece of obsidian. This was assumed that this was the mark or brand of the man to be initiated into the order. The gashes would allow for the blood to flow freely during flagellation and prevent welts, bruises or permanent scars.

Neighboring Moradas often would go visit each other during Holy Week. There were other times that they would get together because it was part of their agreement that they had in their laws to help each other in time of need or if they needed to help each other for some reason they would. If there was any flagellation it would usually take place, dressed before Holy Saturday. La Procession de Sangre (Procession of Blood), does not occur any more. In earlier times the Brothers would walk from the Morada to a close-by Calvario, a large cross erected on a hill representing Mount Calvary. In this procession the Penitentes, dressed only in white cotton drawers. They would whip themselves with plaited yucca whips called disciplinas. The Pitero (fluteplayer) played the small pito while the Brothers sang Alabados. This songs were very old hymns which are reminiscent of the fifteenth and sixteenth-century Spanish songs.

They marched in procession single file. Their heads were always covered. They all wore white short pants and they were barefoot. The whip (cat of nine tails), some had thorns at each end. Every so many steps both arms would rise above their heads and you could hear the lash from afar. Because of the gashes the blood would flow down their backs, drawers and their legs. Some of the Hermanos would carry large wooden crosses, called (Madero's), on their shoulders in emulation of Christ. Each Penitente had one or two helpers to carry him if he became to hurt or weak to continue.

On Good Friday as special exercise, took place. It was called El Encuentro. This is the only part of the Holy Week where women and nonmembers of the Morada were allowed to participate. The women would carry an image of the Virgin Mary from the church into town. Los Hermanos would carry a statue of Christ from their Morada. The two different groups would meet and they would sing Alabados. This would commemorate the meeting of Mary and Jesus on the Via Dolorosa. Many times there were men who would take the part of Jesus and he would also carry a large cross.

The Ultimate part is the Crucifixion, it would take place on Good Friday. One Hermano would be chosen to represent Christ. He would come from the Morada at a certain time, wearing a hood. This was done to have his identity as a penance and not a matter of who he was or his pride. A majority of the Penitentes would wear masks for the same reason during public processions. The Christ is laid on the cross and his arms and legs were bound to it with rope. The cross would be pulled upright and the Hermano would be there until the ropes cut of his circulation causing unconsciousness. The Hermanos would remove the man by cutting off the ropes and would take the man into the Morada where they would revive him.

All during lent, but particularly during Holy Week, there was torture and blood. When the holy season was over, some of the Hermanos ended up in bed. A lot of the Hermanos were so pale and wasted from lack of sleep, the sacrifices, the self-denial to their own bodies took their due. One certainly has to have a fierce and fighting faith in order to suffer the similar torment that Christ did. The Penitentes endured pain and suffering that most humans would not be able to endure.

People attended their public ceremonies like attending a game, a spectacle or a bullfight. Blood has always excited the people. Everyone watched with awe, they trembled, and soon forgot what they had just witnessed. That ferocious reality was so extreme that it almost looked unreal, as if it was not really happening at all. There are many stories that in the olden days, they would hang a Penitente on the cross and leave him hanging there for three hours during the passion and death of our Lord. This I never saw, and for that I give thanks to God. People often ask if nails were ever used in these crucifixions. I have no authentic eye-witness of nails, ever being used, but this of course, does not rule out the possibility that it didn't ever happen. This is not to say that men have not died on the cross or from inflicted self-whipping. The Lenten season for Southern Colorado and Northern New Mexico usually has pretty cold weather wise. I remember Holy Week always being windy and cold. Physical punishment, exposure to the whipping's, loss of blood could easily weaken anybody enough to cause them to die.

The real climax of the Penitente Holy Week always happened on Good Friday night when Las Tinieblas (ignorance, and fear) was celebrated. This service, based on the Catholic Tenebrae re-enacts the darkness and confusion when Christ was put on the cross to die. They would always allow all the family to attend. Women, children and everyone else from the village that wanted to attend. In front of the Alter stood a candle holder with thirteen candles, which stood for Christ, and the twelve Apostles. They would sing Alabados and they would pray and recite different psalms. When they finished each set one candle was extinguished. When all twelve candles were out, the main candle, the Christ, was removed to another room and the Morada would be in total darkness. The Hermanos Penitentes would break up into screaming, and Matracas (wooden ratchet) would rattle and this would go on as they would continue the disciplinas to their backs. They would pray for their Village, all that had deceased and for all the families.

The Tinieblas of Holy Week would be over for the Hermano Penitentes. Holy Saturday was very quiet and all the women would make lots of festive food. The Easter service was done by a priest from the Catholic Church when I was a child. When it first started in the 18th century the secret society, the Hermano Mayor would be in charge.

The actual rituals that took place from one village to another were basically the same in every little village. The Hermano Penitentes were the ones that organized their own laws for their individual Morada. As far as I know there were no written laws or who could join to become a Hermano of their Village. Anyone could join if they were males and the had strong beliefs and faith of how Christ lived. The Hermanos Penitentes existed in every Village and their rules, rituals, customs were varied from one village to another. They each had their own Morada and they were very proud to be Hermano Penitentes of their Villages. Though self-flagellation was never the main theme of the Hermano Penitentes, it did exist. However, those practices were restricted and carried out in strict privacy. To be able to separate the facts from pure myths of the past is very difficult. During the 1930's attempts were made to document that the Hermano Penitentes did exist. They did make the Hermano Penitentes a non-profit organization which is governed under the church in Santa Fe, New Mexico. In New Mexico there are Hermano Penitentes in Rio Arriba, Mora, Taos and San Miguel counties. In Southern Colorado they existed in the San Luis Valley. There are leaders from the Morada that go to Santa Fe to meet with the Archbishop and other officials of the church. There are different stories of when the Penitentes really started but there is evidence from my Great-Grandparents that they existed in Los Sauces, Colorado in 1830. The Hermano Penitentes, did become visible, after Mexico got its independence from Spain. The Franciscans had taken care of the spiritual needs for New Mexico which the San Luis Valley was part of that. The people were forced to take over all religious, except whatever was assigned to the priests. The priests were in charge of Baptisms, burials and any other religious ceremonies and all the holy days the people of the villages were in charge. At this time, it became the responsibility of the Hermano Penitentes to keep the religion alive. My Great-Grand Father always said the self-flagellation came from Spain. This did not come from the Indians that were here.

While everything was drastically changing in America, there was an influx of Anglo's which were predominantly Protestant. In 1851 New Mexico was awarded its first Catholic Bishop, Jean Lamy, who was French and came to the west from the East. He never quite understood what the Penitente Brotherhood really stood for and he felt threatened that they would hurt the Catholics. The Anglos that came from the East could not distinguish between the Hermano Penitentes and Catholics. With all this happening in the region the Bishop forbade the Hermano Penitentes from doing their Rituals. At that time the Hermano Penitentes went underground. They would have never survived the Anglos who were making Penitente Watching like a sport just to make fun of them. All the ridicule they inhibited upon them made them go into increased secrecy.

In January 28, 1947, the Archbishop Byrne, acknowledged the Hermano Penitentes as a society of Men that were within the Catholic Church. The Hermano Penitentes got the blessings of the archbishop if they existed in moderation, and the guidance of the Catholic Church.

I have truly enjoyed doing all the research and trying to remember what my Great-Grandparents have taught me. This was a way of living in this small villages and it truly inspires me to think that they were the government and backbone of our history and how we lived and learned to live.

THE PENITENTES INFLUENCE

Among the things which shape our lives, perhaps our history is the most significant. Yet it is often the least understood. Schools and books attempt to define our history in terms of George Washington, John F. Kennedy, and other similarly distant factors. Surely these persons and places contributed to our history, but their role in our lives is a very minor one. We must begin to look closer to home. We must acknowledge the people who really influenced our lives more than anyone. We must look closer to home. We must honor those who gave us our names and who have fashioned for us a history as beautiful and rich as it is obscure. Each story we tell, each song we sing, becomes part of this magnificent history we have to share.

GLOSSARY

ACOMPANADOR: A brother who aids another Penitente brother who needs help during their public appearance.

Alabado: a religious hymn

Calvario: A large wooden cross used by the Hermano Penitentes during lent and holy week.

Calzones: white undergarments worn during their Penance time.

Disciplina: A whip made of yucca fibers, used for self-flagellation:

Los Hermanos: The brotherhood

Hermano Mayor: He was an elected official of the Morada.

Matraca: A wooden rachet or noisemaker, used during holy week during the services in place of bells.

Morada: The adobe or stone house used by the Hermano Penitentes.

Penitentes: brotherhood

Pitero: The flute player

Pito: A small wooden piece of wood used to play music.

Rezador: One who reads, prays or chats the Penitente Services.

Sangrador: One who makes slashes on the Penitentes.

ABOUT THE AUTHOR

I am Janice A. Martinez de Valdez. Born and raced in Los Sauces, Colorado. I grew up in a wonderful ranch-farm owned by my parents. Jose Faustin Martinez and Maria Sophia Montoya. I used to spend a lot of time with my grandparents. My paternal grandparents were Alfredo Martinez, and Matilde Marquez de Martinez. Maternal grandparents, Pedro J. Montoya, and Cleotilde Medina de Montoya. I knew everyone that lived in Los Sauces at a very young age. I often visited with all the elderly and did chores for them. To me I always greeted them as Aunt or Uncle.

I graduated from Sanford High School, I received my BA degree from Adams State University, my MA from the University of New Mexico, and I have lots of post degree education also. I retired from teaching from the state of New Mexico. After retiring from teaching I took care of my husband for fifteen years, He was Gregorio Jake Valdez, we had two beautiful sons, Joaquin A. Valdez, and Jake A. Valdez III. My husband was a Vietnam Veteran who came back home from Vietnam with a lot of physical problems. We were married almost forty years. He passed away just short of that. My youngest son was killed on an accident. That was a devastating loss to me and will always be. I have five grandchildren from Joaquin and Melanie Duran Valdez. They have become the center of my life. I have taken care of them for the past twelve years.

I have always had this desire to write a book about the penitentes. They shaped the lives of many and have not been given the credit they so humbly deserve. I truly Love our culture and rich values our Hispanic people have. I believe this book I have written speaks to the relevance the

Penitentes have in shaping our lives in so many ways.

God has blessed me in so many ways I want to thank him for giving me this beautiful opportunity of being able to write this book." I would like to thank all my family and friends who have supported me in this endeavor. God Bless You!!!

Made in the USA
Middletown, DE
07 December 2022